Out of Control

Written by **Fiona Undrill**

Illustrated by **Russ Daff**

OXFORD
UNIVERSITY PR

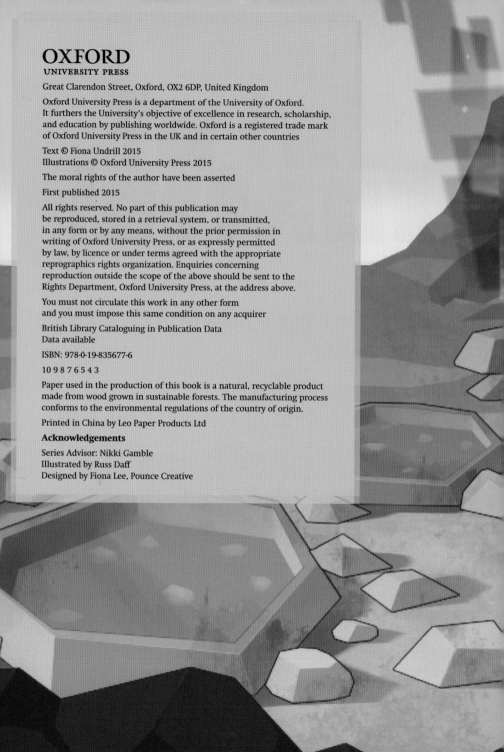

OXFORD
UNIVERSITY PRESS

Great Clarendon Street, Oxford, OX2 6DP, United Kingdom

Oxford University Press is a department of the University of Oxford.
It furthers the University's objective of excellence in research, scholarship,
and education by publishing worldwide. Oxford is a registered trade mark
of Oxford University Press in the UK and in certain other countries

British Library Cataloguing in Publication Data
Data available

ISBN: 978-0-19-835677-6

10 9 8 7 6 5 4 3

Paper used in the production of this book is a natural, recyclable product
made from wood grown in sustainable forests. The manufacturing process
conforms to the environmental regulations of the country of origin.

Printed in China by Leo Paper Products Ltd

Acknowledgements

Series Advisor: Nikki Gamble
Illustrated by Russ Daff
Designed by Fiona Lee, Pounce Creative

CHAPTER 1

The space shuttle spun wildly. It was completely out of control and there was nothing Jake could do. He watched in horror as the shuttle crash-landed into a crater.

"Not again!" Jake sighed. *Space Explorers* was a brilliant game but it was *very* difficult. Jake's big brother Sam was really good at it, and Jake was determined to become as good as him.

Jake had often watched Sam play, wishing he could get as far into the game as his brother. He knew that landing Marco's space shuttle was just the beginning. You had to land on lots of different planets and get Marco to collect rock samples.

There was one planet, Planet Kapton, that had an incredible castle. That was where Jake wanted to take Marco. But Jake couldn't even land the shuttle safely on Kapton's bumpy surface.

Jake felt someone sit down beside him.

"*Space Explorers* is too hard for you,"
Sam said.

"No, it's *not*!" Jake protested.

Mum looked up. "Maybe Sam could help you, Jake?" she suggested.

"*No!*" Sam complained. "Jake's time is up. It's my turn to play now."

Mum checked her watch. "He's right, Jake. Sorry."

"It's not fair," Jake sighed, and he trudged up to his room.

Jake pulled out his plastic bricks. Sam
was amazing at video games, but Jake was
an awesome builder. His latest castle was his
best yet!

Jake worked on the staircase that wound
around his castle and tried to forget about how
mean Sam was being about *Space Explorers*.

CHAPTER 2

"This time I'll land Marco safely," Jake thought the following day. He was desperate to explore Planet Kapton's glowing castle.

It was hard to concentrate with the constant thumping of Sam's tennis ball against the wall of the house.

"I can't concentrate on *Space Explorers* when you're doing that!" Jake shouted out of the window to Sam.

"It's too difficult for you, anyway!" Sam shouted back.

Soon, despite the noise, Jake was concentrating hard on the game.

Jake began by memorizing the flight controls. He zoomed Marco's shuttle through some practice flights until he felt ready for the mission.

"Come on," Jake told himself, wriggling on the sofa. "You can do it." The abandoned alien castle was glowing on the planet below.

Jake flew the shuttle down and it landed with a bump. But Marco was safe! Then Jake controlled Marco, making him jump out of the shuttle to explore.

Small purple aliens popped out from the castle's steaming yellow moat and surrounded Marco. With playful squeaks, they started to follow him.

"They're tiny!" laughed Jake, and he made Marco leap over them. But they were fast. Jake raced Marco across the bridge to the gate and slammed it shut, leaving the aliens squeaking outside.

"Now where?" Jake wondered.

Ahead, there was a massive doorway. Jake took Marco through it and found a corridor lined with hundreds of arched doors. But which one should Jake send Marco through? He looked at the pictures above the doors for clues.

WHOOSH!

Suddenly, a trapdoor flew open beneath Marco's feet.

Marco fell, spinning down ... and Jake felt as if *he* was spinning, too.

"Woah, that's a *weird* feeling!" said Jake.

"I thought so, too," Marco replied.

"What?" gasped Jake. "What happened?" He gazed around, totally confused. He wasn't in the living room! He was in the castle! *With Marco!*

"You were the one controlling the game,"
said Marco. "You tell me."

"But ... how ...?" Jake spluttered in confusion.

"You want to know how to get out?"
Marco interrupted. "The exit's through there."
He pointed towards a door. "And hurry!
Those smaller aliens were harmless but the
others will be here any minute."

Jake didn't hesitate. He burst through the door –
then grabbed on to the door frame. Between this
door and the exit were stepping stones. There
were **enormous** gaps between them – and
below was a lake of bubbling red lava.

"Take these," said Marco, and he handed Jake a pair of boots with springs on them.

With the springy boots on, Jake bounded swiftly across the stepping stones.

Jake reached the final stepping stone and jumped triumphantly through the exit.

CHAPTER 3

Suddenly, Jake found himself back on the sofa, dizzy and puzzled. What had just happened?

"Was I really in the game?" he thought. He shook his head. "Not possible." But it had been so much fun!

"Did you give up?" said Sam, suddenly appearing.

"What do you mean?" asked Jake.

"I looked through the window and you weren't here," said Sam. "I thought you'd had enough of the game and gone to build castles."

"No ..." Jake began. He wanted to say more but he was too busy trying to work out what had just happened. If Sam thought he had gone to his room earlier, *had* he been in the game?

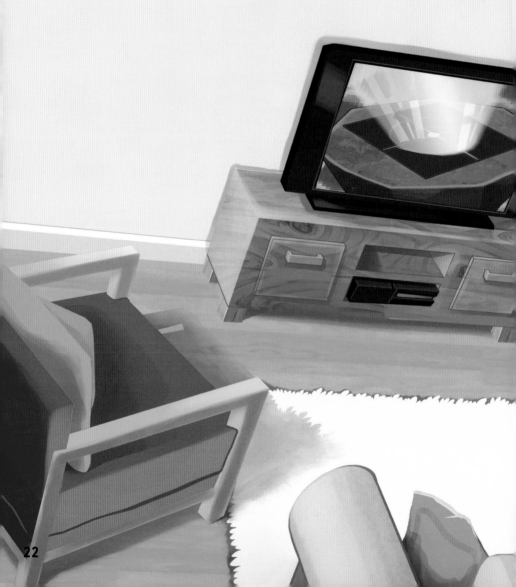

"Move over," said Sam, nudging Jake. "Let me show you how it's done."

"But I'm not finished," cried Jake.

"It's my turn," said Sam. "We're supposed to take turns."

Reluctantly, Jake let Sam have the controls and plodded up to his room.

CHAPTER 4

After school the next day, Jake couldn't wait to get back to Planet Kapton.

He landed the shuttle with a few gentle bumps and hopped Marco over the little purple aliens. Then he made Marco go through the gate, over to the corridor with the doors, and onto the trapdoor.

Once more, Jake felt himself spinning and once more, he found himself with Marco.

"You again?" Marco asked.

"Me again," replied Jake.

They were in some sort of gallery.

"I'm seriously glad that these aliens have abandoned this castle," Jake thought.

The portraits alone gave him goosebumps.

Jake suddenly felt nervous.

"Marco," he asked, "if I'm here, *in the game*, does that mean I'm not at home anymore?"

"Well, you can't be in two places at once, can you?" Marco reasoned.

"I guess not," Jake answered.

"So you need to be careful," Marco
continued, "because if you get stuck here ..."

"I'll never get home again!" breathed Jake.

"Exactly. You got out last time but
it won't always be so easy."

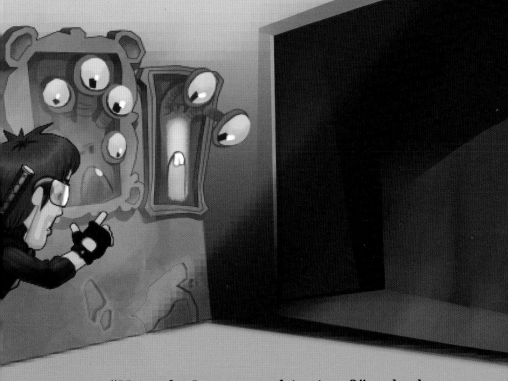

"How do I get out this time?" asked
Jake, suddenly worried.

Marco pointed down a dark hallway.
"That way. But look out for Astrobull!"

Jake ran down the hallway and found himself in a maze. He liked mazes in video games ... usually. But right now he could hear a menacing roar coming from around one of the corners.

"That must be **Astrobull**," Jake thought, "and he doesn't sound very friendly!"

Jake swung around corners, smashed against dead ends and slammed into walls. This wasn't like any maze he had tackled before. He wondered what would happen if Astrobull caught him. It was only a game ... wasn't it?

He was about to find out.
Jake felt Astrobull's hot breath on his neck as the monster let out a **mighty roar**.

At last, Jake saw the trapdoor exit.
"I must … get there … before Astrobull …
reaches me!" he panted. He sprinted to
the exit, leaped onto the trapdoor and
fell through.

He made it!

Jake crashed back onto the sofa, his head spinning. This was the *most* exciting video game *ever*! That's if it *was* a game. What would have happened if Astrobull had caught him? Jake shuddered.

CHAPTER 5

"Where's Sam?" Mum asked later.

"Playing *Space Explorers?*" suggested Jake.

"No, he was in the living room earlier," replied Mum, "but he's not there now. I can't find him anywhere."

Jake shrugged and kept working on his castle.

"Honestly, you two keep disappearing; I lost you for half an hour yesterday, too!" Mum said.

Jake's hand froze. "Perhaps Sam has entered the game," he thought.

"It's not like Sam to go off somewhere without telling me," Mum worried. "It's over an hour since I saw him."

"An hour!" Jake's heart pounded frantically. What if Sam was trapped in the game … **forever?**

"He's probably playing tennis," Jake said,
trying to stay cool.

Mum peered anxiously out of the window.
"I'll have another look."

Jake hurtled downstairs. He
grabbed the controls, launched
Marco through the trapdoor and
spun into the game.

CHAPTER 6

This time, Jake and Marco tumbled into a garden.

"Ouch!" grumbled Marco. "That's twice today! And neither of you are any help with finding rocks. Look at my crates – nearly all of them are empty!"

"Twice?" Jake asked, hurriedly. "So you've seen my brother?"

"Looks like you, but bigger?" asked Marco.

Jake nodded.

"He's trapped," said Marco. "Perhaps this game is too hard for him."

Yesterday, that comment would have made Jake smile.

"You'd better get out before you get trapped, too," Marco advised. "The game is getting harder."

"But I have to save Sam!" Jake shouted.

"That might be tricky. He's up there." Marco pointed to a tall tower.

Jake walked around the tower. There was no door!

"How do I get up to the window?" Jake frowned.

"Climb?" Marco suggested.

Jake ran his hand along the tower
wall. It was too smooth and too steep to climb.
Frustrated, Jake kicked Marco's pile of empty
crates. One clattered to the ground.

"Of course!" thought Jake.

They could build their way up – using crates!

Jake and Marco rapidly built a staircase up the tower.

As they got closer, Jake called, **"Sam! I'm coming!"**

Sam's surprised face poked out of the window.

"Jake!" he cried with relief. "Quick!"

Finally, Jake reached the window. Sam clambered out and they scrambled down the stairs.

"Which way now?" asked Jake desperately.

Marco pointed towards two big doors. "That way!" he said. "Be careful!"

They opened the doors and were immediately blasted by icy snowballs. Jake slammed the doors shut.

"We'll never get across there!" Jake yelled.
"Now we're *both* stuck here."

"Stuck in the *game*?" panicked Sam.
"That's impossible!"

"It *is* possible and we *have* to get out,"
Jake cried urgently.

"Take this," said Marco, holding up
his backpack.

Sam didn't hesitate. He grabbed a shovel
from the pack.

"Come on!" he yelled, charging through
the doors.

The snowballs were flying straight at them,
but Sam skilfully whacked the icy missiles
away as if they were tennis balls.

Eventually, covered in ice, Sam and Jake jumped onto the trapdoor exit and spun back home.

CHAPTER 7

The brothers landed clumsily back on the sofa.

"That was scary!" Jake exclaimed. "Thanks for getting us through."

"Thanks for rescuing me," said Sam. "That game is **out of control!**"

"I hope Marco's OK," said Jake.

Sam laughed. "He's just a video game character, Jake!"

Suddenly, there was a thud as a third
body landed on the sofa.

The boys gasped.

"You could have waited," puffed Marco.

Marco dusted the snow from his
clothes. "You didn't think I was
staying in *there*, did you?"